A NEW SONG

The Last Years of Chris's Life

By Pat Montesano

authorHOUSE®

AuthorHouse™
1663 Liberty Drive
Bloomington, IN 47403
www.authorhouse.com
Phone: 1-800-839-8640

First published by AuthorHouse 06/24/2011

ISBN: 978-1-4634-1164-0 (ebk)
ISBN: 978-1-4634-1165-7 (hc)
ISBN: 978-1-4634-1166-4 (sc)

Library of Congress Control Number: 2011908869

Printed in the United States of America

Dedicated To All Who
Are Developmentally Disabled
and Their Families

A Note of Thanks

Several years ago, after having my first book published about the childhood of my son Chris, I met a retired priest friend at the grocery store whom I hadn't seen in many months. The elderly white-haired man stopped me by the meat counter, and told me he had read my book in which I had told the intimate story of our family raising a handicapped child. His eyes filled with tears as he told me that in all of his life he had not understood children and people who suffered from mental retardation, and confessed he had always been afraid of them.

"Until I read your book," Father told me, "I didn't realize these individuals actually have feelings. As I read your book I did laugh and cry for all of you, but I also cried for myself for not accepting these special people into my life when I had the opportunities."

He then thanked me for writing SING A NEW SONG and for giving him new awareness in his old age.

For a long time, I thought of that meeting in the grocery store and of the gratitude I felt for touching that one life with my book. It had been very hard to expose my feelings, those of my family, those of Chris, and those of my deceased husband to all my readers. It had been difficult to recall memories of those years. The old priest thanking me gave such meaning to having written that first book about Chris.

Years later this same elderly priest was terminally ill and in the last days of his life in a local nursing home. It just so happened that Chris was, at the time, volunteering at that nursing home and spent time at Father's bedside, sitting with him and talking with him.....at the dying priest's request.

~~~

A year after Chris died, I was preparing to leave a Thanksgiving dinner given by the Faith and Light organization Chris had belonged to. As I walked towards the door with some of my children and grandchildren, a woman approached me with her adult handicapped son.

"Pat," she said, as she introduced herself, "I'm Lorraine. I have hoped to meet you for many years. I want to thank you for writing your first book about Chris. I also read your second book about him, but it was the first one you wrote that helped me to raise my son."

I was speechless! I could only stare at her as she continued.

"I used to lie in bed crying in frustration, holding your book, and telling God, 'If Pat could do it, I can too.'"

Her son stood there smiling and nodding to me the entire time she spent thanking me. I had such a lump in my throat that all I could say was "Thank You" to Lorraine. There it was again: My very reason for writing about Chris is in hope of touching one person, or helping one other parent. I had such a lump rising in my throat that all I could say was, "Thank you. Thank you."

Some parents had asked me, after Chris's death, if I would write a last book about him. I had gone to a Faith & Light retreat soon after he died, and the parents there had asked me to write one more book about him. I thought there was no way I could do it, but being approached by Lorraine after the Faith & Light dinner gave me the motivation I needed. It has been difficult writing, but I hope there will be someone "out there" who might find some help or consolation in our story....maybe hope. Most of all I want to touch hearts with the knowledge that the life of my son was of remarkable value.

It has taken me over two years to write this book, and there was a time when I got totally discouraged and stopped writing it. One day during that period I decided to look on Amazon. com to see if SING A NEW SONG II was still selling, and I found very favorable comments from readers of my books. There was a beautiful comment by Lorraine. What a surprise! There again was the motivation I needed to continue, and there again.... those words filling my heart: Thank You!

~~~

Two years ago my 18th grandchild was born. During her second high-risk pregnancy my daughter, Rosemary, had expressed fears to her doctor of something going wrong during childbirth and she worried about the loss of oxygen for her baby. She shared with me the assuring information her doctor gave her about Cool Caps, which I had never heard of. These are devises to prevent damage in newborns due to oxygen deprivation Chris suffered from loss of oxygen during birth, and the resulting brain damage was shown to us on film after extensive testing when he was 12. Most of his special friends through the years had suffered from the same misfortune:

brain damage resulting from oxygen deprivation during birth. Hearing about the FDA-approved device that can save infants from brain damage is so amazing to me! I am very grateful to know that research was able to accomplish this! I have been reading articles about cool caps on the internet. I find it so fascinating!

The following excerpts are from a CBS News article of 12/21/2006:

> "It doesn't take long for brain cells deprived of oxygen to begin to die," she (Dr. Emily Senay) said. 'If that process cannot be held to a minimum, the damage to the brain can be permanent.... leading to lifelong problems like blindness, cerebral palsy, and mental retardation."

> "Because the brain and the infant's entire body are so fragile and vulnerable, the cooling needs to occur gently, with great care taken that the baby's body temperature doesn't drop below about 94 degrees Fahrenheit...going any lower can be life threatening. So this new device doesn't just circulate cooled water. It also includes electrodes to precisely monitor the temperature

of the water and of the baby, and a single channel electroencephalogram to keep a close eye on brain activity during the procedure."

Now there is a video available entitled *COOL CAP FOR NEWBORNS* at http://www.youtube.com/watch?v=HiBCJ5g_FW4. You can hear the narrator explaining there has been a 60% reduction in cerebral palsy in infants who have gone without oxygen and are treated with these cool caps within 6 hours after birth. The decrease of inflammation and swelling of the brain by freezing works to avoid brain damage. Water pumped through channels to cool the brain lowers the baby's temperature 6 or 7 degrees, slowing down harmful injury-causing chemicals and washing those chemicals away. At this time the cap is worn for approximately 72 hours.

Chris's life has been of such tremendous value to all of us in my family, but it is good news to know that many babies can now be saved from such a hard life. For Chris and all his special friends, as well as thousands of others, who have actually contributed to this research by their very births and lives, those words are always alive in my heart: Thank you!

My constant reminder of the beauty and value of those special lives comes to me every holiday, on my birthday and

Mother's Day, in a phone call from Chris's handicapped friend, Tommy, a man in his 50's who lives alone with his dog. Tommy's sister oversees his care with the help of counselors.

"Hi Pat," he happily greets me, before giving me his best wishes for the day and its celebration. He wants to know what I'm doing for the occasion and tells me of his plans.

After we have a conversation he always ends with, "You know why I call you, right?

It's for my friend, Chris."

TABLE OF CONTENTS

" It turned out Chris spent his last years in a beautiful spot,

and enjoyed it there

getting to know the birds,

the deer,

rabbits,

foxes,

and the bears."

Frank Montesano, Chris's Brother

CHAPTER 1

From Rosary Beads to Crucifix

Chris lay motionless on the floor when his older brother, Frank, found him next to his bed. Frank had been awakened by a loud thud and ran into his younger brother's room. He quickly began calling out to Chris who opened his eyes and appeared startled.

"I'm ok, Frank. I'm ok," he kept saying as Frank helped his brother sit up and then sit on the side of the bed. Frank got him some water and spent time with him until he felt comfortable letting him go back to sleep. The following morning Frank called me and told me about the incident and that it had happened a few times previously at their mountain home.

"Mom, I think we need to take him to a neurologist again. Something's wrong, and I think he's having seizures again, though I haven't seen that."

Frank had been Chris's caretaker for about 12 years and

truly led Chris to what I was seeing as the peak of his life so far. By buying their trailer home at the edge of Rocky Mountain National Forest and introducing Chris to many species of birds, various wonders of nature including a visiting Mama Bear and cubs; Frank had given Chris more happiness and independence than he had never known. Frank taught him all about the birds and they named those who came daily to be fed. He taught him the different types of trees surrounding them, and Chris was delighted and excited when a new tree sprang up from the ground. Wildflowers were a treat for him, and he learned their names also. He walked the dirt road, about a mile, each day to get their mail; while getting acquainted with neighbors along the way. There were some who welcomed him and conversed with him, even invited him into their homes; while others were not comfortable with a disabled man who spoke with speech impediment, was hearing impaired, and suffered from mental retardation. There were some who withdrew from him as he approached, hand extended and smiling in anticipation of introducing himself. He had learned through his lifetime of similar experiences to seemingly dismiss such rejections from his mind, shrug his shoulders, and continue on his way. Outside our family, he had often been laughed at, ridiculed, and rejected. Inside our family we tried to show him that such behavior wasn't acceptable as we focused on praising him, including him, and loving him unconditionally. At Chris's graduation from a private residential school for children with multiple handicaps when he was 15, a girl who suffered from Down Syndrome gave a speech. "I have learned here that when someone calls me 'stupid'," she told us, "I will think in my mind, 'No, you are stupid for saying that to me,' but I will be kind and not say that."

As an adult Chris was handling rejection quietly and with grace.

In this happy time of new awareness for Chris, Frank feared seizures were occurring after a lapse of 20 years. Chris had not been prescribed seizure medication for all that time. We took him to a neurologist who ran tests and prescribed lab work, and quickly came to the conclusion that Chris was experiencing nocturnal seizures which explained why Frank could only suspect they were occurring. The pleasant, reassuring, young physician talked to Chris about taking medicine for seizure activity again and my son shrugged his shoulders and simply replied, "OK"

So he was going back on the medication, Dilantin, which had weakened and damaged his gums from its use as a child until it was decided he didn't need it any more in his early twenties. His breath had grown increasingly foul smelling through that period, and nothing we tried helped much. My other 7 children and their spouses were constantly telling him to brush his teeth as the problem worsened. After many, many years of this difficulty a nurse told me the only way to solve the dental hygiene problem for my 43-year-old son would be to pull all of his teeth which were quite loose in his diseased gums, and to get him dentures. When I took him to an oral surgeon he told me the problem had most likely been caused by the Dilantin he had taken for several years. He explained that he would extract all of Chris's teeth in his office, at one time. Soon afterward the new dentures would be put in.

Not long afterward, following several dental visits of preparation, Chris's teeth were removed as Frank and I sat in the waiting room. When Chris appeared, he was quite pale and bleeding somewhat, but managed a huge smile for us. Both he and Frank were ready to go home where Frank would care for him. The adjustment to the dentures took several months as he tried to adapt to talking, chewing, and eating. Frank felt good about the way he nursed his brother who was 3 years younger than he. He played the songs Chris liked on the CD player during the recovery period. When Frank asked him what music he wanted, he almost always told him,

"Beatles. George." In the past, the two of them would sing George Harrison's song, "If I Needed Someone," along with the tape blasting away. Chris almost always chose that song to listen to as he healed.

Chris had a fear of the dentures falling out and would ask his brothers to bring him "glue for the teeth" whenever they called. His top dresser drawer grew full of tubes of the adhesive, next to his stack of hearing aid batteries, squeezing all his socks into a corner of the drawer. We joked about Chris being part-owner of the Polygrip company.

He was spending less time making Rosary Beads for poor people of the church, because he found it very difficult to keep track of the 10 beads to be assembled 5 times and separated by 1 large bead. The process got him increasingly frustrated and angry with himself for not being able to make the prayer beads correctly. One day he called me to come and get all the Rosary Beads because he was "finished making them for the poor people." When I arrived he hurriedly got the shoe box full of the Rosary Beads and leftover string and beads. He smiled broadly when he told me, "I hope your friend at the church will like them."

I delivered the box to Addy with the Rosary Beads containing huge knots tied throughout and decades of 13 or 6 beads instead of the required 10, and beads of all different sizes and colors. The only thing done perfectly was the fastening of a cross on each one. I quietly handed Addy the box at church, and she smiled and thanked me. She kindly asked if my son needed more materials to make more Rosary Beads. I responded that he didn't feel up to the project at this time, and she politely thanked me and asked me to thank him.

The experience had its rewards though: His sister, Donna, brought Chris a big case full of multi-colored beads of all sizes and shapes, divided in small compartments. She asked him to make her a necklace and also make some for anyone else he would like to. He had a wonderful time stringing the beads in many creative ways, with sizes, colors, and shapes differing but looking fine. He would tie just one big knot at the end, and he thoroughly enjoyed the new project. He made necklaces for all the females in our family; sisters, sisters-in-law, nieces, and grand-nieces. Some special friends got them too. He gave me 2 necklaces, explaining he had chosen colors to go with some outfits I had at the time. He was very pleased with the many necklaces, and we all found them to be special and quite pretty.

The beading of necklaces was a wonderful project during the cold winter months in the old trailer. Frank and Chris were often snowed in, with a few feet of snow surrounding the trailer and the ice-laden trees of the forest looming all around. Frank would turn the oven up to 500 degrees to help keep the place warm, and small electric heaters were plugged in to warm the different rooms. Sometimes ice formed on the inside of the windows, which caused Chris to laugh heartily.

"Look at this, Frank," he would say while laughing, "ice in our house."

One blustery snow day I drove to the trailer and found my sons wearing parkas and knit hats inside the trailer to keep warm. Frank was laughing about seeing their breath it was so cold in there..

"Frank says we have to wear coats and hats in here today," Chris laughed.

Chris liked to sit watching Frank work on the computer. He would offer advice at times also, which Frank found amusing. However, Chris had a habit of humming in a monotone when he was sitting there. We knew he couldn't hear himself, but everyone around him always heard the continuous sound. Frank found it hard to ignore when working on the computer or watching tv shows and movies with his brother. So music, and tv sounds were often on high volume to drown out Chris's humming. Of course, the louder the better for Chris in his deafness, but it left the rest of us wide-eyed!

Often there were power outages at the trailer, so Frank kept a good supply of candles on hand. Chris couldn't understand why Christmas candles were burning when it wasn't Christmas. He thought that was funny too. There would be great jubilation when power returned and music played again, and all was warm and well lit at their home in the woods.

Frank would often cook up a big meal of spaghetti and meatballs to celebrate. Chris also liked the chili Frank made on cold winter days, and the soups cooking in the big pot on the old stove. Sometimes there was venison stew made with the meat their brother, Paul, provided from hunting.

Frank always made sure that Chris got to his monthly Faith and Light meetings, no matter what the weather was. Usually he stayed with me at my apartment following the meetings. It was on one of those cold winter nights when I opened my door to Chris returning from his meeting with a big smile on his face. He quickly handed me a small crucifix he had made at his meeting, before even entering my apartment.

"I made it for you, Mom!"

It was made of clothespins and his name was printed on it. He was beaming with pride and happiness. I immediately hung it on the wall where everyone who entered would see it. Even the figure of Jesus on The Cross was made of a clothespin. Out of the cold night had come this special son of mine with such a special gift for me.

As the hard cold days surrounded them each winter, Frank often reminded Chris that Spring would come soon. In the meantime herds of mule deer visited the property often. . It was truly a beautiful place, especially when the bright sun would shine from the deep blue sky through the ice-covered forest. It was a beautiful world.....and Chris was happy.

CHAPTER 2
Feeding the Birds

Dr. Wayne Dyer (on his PBS specials) likes to use this quotation in his talks: "If you change the way you look at things, the things you look at will change." I think many of us looked at nature differently, more intimately, more appreciatively, through Frank and Chris in their mountain home.

"Look!" Chris would exclaim at a simple acorn or pinecone on the ground. He was excited by simple beauty and reminded us to stop and look.

"Watch out! Watch out!" He would be sure to warn us to stand aside as a rabbit ran past or a chipmunk, or a field mouse. He made sure he protected them.

"Here's Harry! Here comes Harry!" He would excitedly point to a Hairy Woodpecker flying in to eat from one of the many bird feeders Frank had hung all around their home. They hung from trees and posts, and little birdhouses sat perched on various logs and large rocks. Frank had purchased some of the feeders, and friends had given many so that Chris had plenty in order to feed the increasing number of birds arriving each day, year round. The red-winged blackbirds arrived in large throngs. At times there were so many birds that their sound was deafening. I loved to listen to that as well as the chirping of the friendly chickadees.

Chris had a ladder to carry around each morning to climb on and reach the feeders that were hung high. He could be heard talking to the birds, calling them to come for their food. There were a few times when a bird would actually land on his shoulder. He learned that this chore was very important, that the birds could not live without his feeding them, especially during the harsh winters. He also grew interested in the other animals, the mule deer, the rabbits, the bears, the fox; and he wanted to know all about what they ate and how they lived. Why was that Mama Bear eating from the bird feeder? She made him laugh at her antics, trying to open the feeders. One time Frank went out onto the deck to chase her from the garbage can and she came running towards him with a food container stuck on her nose. Chris laughed heartily as he and Frank both ran inside. Frank had been yelling, "Get out of here!" But once the bear lunged towards him, he was yelling, "Never mind! We'll get out of here!" He and Chris were shoving each other inside as fast as they could go. Frank got some wonderful photographs and movies of all the visiting animals. Chris was always jumping up from his chair by Frank's computer, whispering loudly, "Frank! Get the camera!"

The bears sometimes came unnoticed and left bird feeders destroyed and trash cans knocked over. With limited income between the brothers, it was discouraging when the bears ate the birds' food. Frank had made a family website and added to it a plea for help to feed Chris's birds. We wanted to keep enough food supplied so Chris could complete his daily chore of feeding them.

Each year the Audubon Society holds The Backyard Bird Count, and Frank enjoyed signing up and participating in the national event. Chris would look forward to the important weekend with great anticipation and preparation. His part was to go out very early and fill all the feeders. He also had to practice being very quiet so the birds would come to be counted. He was also supposed to help with counting. On a few occasions they excitedly recorded birds that had rarely or never been seen in their region, and participated as Audubon Society contributors of important regional documentation.

One day I arrived to find Frank inside looking out the window and motioning for me to come and look at a special bird outside in the tree. "Here's the bird that always comes to visit Chris!"

Frank had told me about a bird that Chris had made friends with, a bird that came every day and got up close to Chris.

Chris was all smiles as I went slowly and quietly to look out at the large Blue Jay. I whispered, "Yes! Pretty colors!" But Frank was shaking his head. "No," he whispered, "look closely." After a pause he whispered, "Do you see it?" I kept looking but didn't know what he wanted me to see. Finally he told me in a hushed tone, "Mom, look at his beak." As the bird turned his head toward me, I was very surprised.

Oh! How strange! The bird had a very deformed, twisted beak. It was not pretty.

Life must be a bit difficult for that bird, with that disability, I thought.

Chris and the deformed bird seemed drawn to each other.

There were other moments that were not quite as pleasant regarding the birds, such as finding one of them dead every now and then. One summer day the 3 of us sat on the new rustic log bench Chris's brother, Mike, and his son, Michael, had made for Frank and Chris. We were very comfortable enjoying refreshments and talking, appreciating the soft summer breeze.

"Mom!" Frank suddenly whispered as he motioned for Chris not to move. There on a branch nearby settled a lovely Mourning Dove. What a beautiful sight! It was a pretty picture to behold, there with the sunlight bouncing from the aspen trees in front of the evergreen where the bird perched and cooed softly. Everything became still except for the peaceful cooing.

Suddenly! A noisy swoosh! There was the loud cracking of branches and movement of bushes as a huge Coopers Hawk swooped in, greedily grabbed the dove, and carried her off in a flash. It happened so quickly! It was terrible! We were all shaken!

After we sat there in shocked silence Frank finally said, "Well, there's nature for you."

"The big bird got hungry," he explained to Chris, who just smiled weakly and walked away.

I personally felt a bit sick to my stomach.

CHAPTER 3

Brotherly Love

"Frank always tells me 'Good Night," Chris had told me. "He likes to have talks with me too, you know, to plan what we do every day." He then repeated, "He always tells me Good Night, and I always tell him Good Night too."

I recalled that conversation with Chris one very hot summer day as I drove up the winding mountain pass, seeking cooler temperatures where my 2 sons had lived for four years. It had been a hectic work week for me, and I enjoyed the beauty of the mountains as I drove from my city apartment toward their mountain property. While looking forward to a tranquil Saturday immersed in the peacefulness of soft-breeze sounds in their back yard, I enjoyed reflecting on the good life Frank was giving Chris in the rustic setting. I had mentioned to Frank and others lately how it seemed Chris had reached a peak of happiness, good health, and contentment. Frank had replied that his brother seemed to feel secure there.

I absorbed the sun glistening on the pond surrounded by tall grasses and bright wildflowers scattered in every direction as I drove on the dirt road which led from the highway to their home. I slowed as Mama Duck hurriedly led her family across the road in front of me towards the pond, after bursting from the bushes. At the top of the hill I turned slowly and drove down the dirt driveway of the thickly treed property, welcomed by the increasingly loud music blasting from the trailer. As always, I parked facing the trailer and sat with my door open for a few minutes, appreciating the Beatles singing, "Imagine." A chipmunk scampered in front of me as I got out of the car, his mouth full of pink insulation robbed from under the trailer in apparent weatherproofing of his own family home under a shed where he quickly disappeared. After walking up the wooden steps slowly, I stood on the deck briefly absorbing the beauty of the deep green forest against the cloudless bright blue Colorado sky. I walked through the open door calling, "Hello? Anyone home?" No one answered me in the noise of the music, so I shouted louder, "Hello?" When I realized no one was in there, I went back outside and walked around the trailer but didn't see my sons anywhere.

Suddenly, I heard them shouting to me from high on a hill behind the trailer.

"Hey, Mom! We're up here," Frank called, and I saw them both waving from quite a distance. I sat down and waited for them as their voices gradually came closer. As they approached I saw how they were struggling to bring their large old rusty wheelbarrow, loaded with big rocks, down the rugged terrain. Stumbling, slipping, they worked to keep their shovels on top of the load they were balancing as they cautiously and slowly descended the rugged hill. Both were wearing bandanas on their sweaty heads, and both had removed their shirts which were now tied around their waists. They were panting as Frank called out directions for every new step to take in the hiking boots they each wore. Small rocks were continuously loosened by their footsteps and rolled down the hill ahead of them. As they came closer, I saw that their chests were soaked with sweat as they finally reached a flat spot near me where they brought the wheelbarrow to a halt, while grunting and bracing themselves against its heavy weight. Frank was catching his breath while Chris couldn't wait to tell me, between heavy breaths, "We're building a wall!" He slipped a bit and grabbed on to a tree. "We got more rocks for the wall!"

Still breathing hard, Frank handed Chris a big mason jar

of ice water from the picnic table, and they passed it back and forth sharing gulps. Frank then told me how they had been working all week to build a larger back yard. They had hauled many wheelbarrows full of dirt from another part of their yard to fill in the large area. Now they were hauling rocks from far off to build a retaining wall around it. Chris beamed with pride as I walked around looking at what they had accomplished, and praised them for their hard work. Perspiration dripped from his hair on to his face, and he seemed proud to wipe it with the rag Frank handed him.

"Mom, you see the blue bird?" Chris asked. I was confused and asked him where there was a blue bird. He just shrugged his shoulders, probably not hearing me correctly, but Frank replied, "I told you about the Blue Heron we see by the pond sometimes. That's what he's talking about." I responded that I had no idea what a Blue Heron looked like, but hadn't seen any blue birds when I drove past the pond. Frank replied, "Oh, you'd know it if you saw it! It's huge."

I was filled with immense feelings of gratitude watching Chris simply able to participate in the hard work with his brother. He was able to actually get enough grip on the shovel, and found the needed strength to lift the dirt into the wheel barrow, something Frank had taken time to teach him. After a brief rest they began unloading the rocks and adding them to the wall they were building. One by one, Chris would bring the rocks to Frank, who would shave them and wedge them into the wall to fit snugly. Each time a rock was finally secure in its place, Chris would stand back and declare, "That's good, Frank!" Frank would then acknowledge his brother's approval enthusiastically. "We got another one in!"

Chris's shoelace had been untied for most of my visit, causing him to trip every now and then while carrying rocks to Frank. Pointing to the untied shoelace, Frank finally stood up to wait while Chris then bent over to tie his shoe. Chris was annoyed to stop his work, as it took him longer than most to tie a shoe. Once he was done they resumed their work, and I was grateful Chris could tie his shoes.

Although Chris sometimes lost his balance for a moment, or had difficulty getting a good grip on each rock he carried to Frank, the work continued. Whenever Frank stopped to wipe the dripping sweat from his face, Chris pulled his handkerchief out of his pocket and did the same. If Frank pulled up his khaki shorts, Chris did the same with his jean cutoffs. If Frank took a sip of water, Chris took one too. Chris picked up his shovel whenever Frank grabbed his. I filled their ice water jar a few times for them, and stayed to enjoy the lunch Frank had prepared. As the three of us sat at the round picnic table eating our sandwiches, we reminisced about everyone who had visited them and carved their names or initials into the old redwood table. Chris pointed out, laughingly, that Frank's son, Frankie, had carved his initials in two different places. He then showed me the signing of their brothers and sisters, nieces and nephews, as well as friends. We watched the many birds coming and going, finding their nutrition from the sunflower seeds in the bird feeders, and chirping under the table as they grabbed our falling tiny bread crumbs.

My sons ate much faster than I as they were anxious to resume their work. After realizing they planned on working til sundown, I relaxed for a while there at the edge of the deep green lush forest. Then there were quick good-byes and hugs in the midst of important work as gray clouds appeared in the distance. Walking to the front of the trailer, I almost tripped over the scurrying chipmunk running toward the shed with another load of pink insulation. After getting into my car, I slowly breathed in one more deep breath of clear mountain air, inhaling with it the healthy scent of pine.

I drove slowly down the dirt road, wiping away the tears which surprised me in the overwhelming blessings of the day. I had never imagined I would see Chris so happy. I had always wanted him to see himself as a strong man. In this moment my wish was satisfied. This felt like a real moment of answered prayer.

While passing the pond I looked for the large blue bird they had talked about, but didn't see it. I actually stopped the car to be sure I wasn't missing the sight of such a big blue bird, but saw only the family of ducks swimming.

As I continued driving I wondered: How many parents get to experience so much gratitude for the hard labor of sons in their forties? How many parents are privileged to be so filled with appreciation for such unconditional love between adult sons? How many mothers are overwhelmed with tears to know a grown son was able to work a shovel and tie his shoes? The sweat, the dirt, the rocks, the baggy shorts, hiking boots, and bandanas had deep meaning for me. It was a precious snapshot that arrived that beautiful summer day in the mountains........ to settle and live in my memory.

Chapter 4

Computers and Puzzles

There was pounding on my apartment door and the sound of Frank and Chris calling me. I quickly opened the door to let them in, Chris leading as he carried a huge heavy piece of wood under a cloth. Frank was behind him, helping to hold the wood up. As soon as they were in my apartment, they unveiled the large puzzle picture Chris had made for me.

"It's for you, Mom! I made it for you!" he said breathlessly and excitedly. "I cut the wood too!" He was so proud of what he had done for me! It didn't matter to any of us that the 22" x 33" piece of wood was ragged where he had sawed it apart from a larger piece of wood. It didn't matter, either, that it was crooked or that the staining wasn't perfect underneath the puzzle. He had done it all by himself in the many hours it took him with all his handicaps.

IT WAS BEAUTIFUL!

Frank quickly got a hammer and nails and put them into my kitchen wall where they then hung the picture of various pastas, jars of Italian foods, kitchen tools, and colorful bowls of cheeses and vegetables. He had put together 500 puzzle pieces to make this picture for me, with hands quite twisted from arthritis. We all stood back to look at it on the wall and to be sure it was safe and straight. (It was very heavy!) . The three of us stood looking at it for a few minutes. Then Chris asked, "You like it, Mom?"

He would really never know how much it meant to me, but I told him how very much I loved it, and that he had done a wonderful job. I really don't know who was more proud: Frank or Chris.

From that day forward, for many months, Chris made puzzles on sawed wood for others in the family. He would call and keep me posted on each project. He had, for all his life, loved putting puzzles together. Now he was enjoying choosing puzzles for family members and then making each into a project to present to them. Everything he did took him much longer than it takes most people, but it was the gift idea that kept him at it, regardless of pain in his hands or his back as he leaned over his projects. I had once taken him to a chiropractor who told me my son was always in pain, but there was nothing he could do to help him. Chris also wore heavy eyeglasses (he was legally blind without them) which often slipped down on his nose and he had to keep pushing them back up.. He hardly ever complained..

As winter approached that year, Frank explained to Chris he should not start another puzzle because it would be too cold to go outside and saw, cut, glue, etc.

"Let's save that for warmer weather."

Instead Frank proceeded to teach Chris how to play games on the computer. He loved it! He especially enjoyed trying to play poker games. So when Frank went to his computer to work on some online computer classes, Chris went to his computer and played games. We all enjoyed him telling us on the phone, "We're busy on our computers."

Frank was always seeking ways to stimulate Chris's motivation and interest. He had always believed that Chris was capable of more than had been predicted for him, accepting the limitations that existed but trying to create new interests and new goals for his brother.

He set up an email account on his computer for Chris and then invited family and friends to email him. Chris would hear, "You have mail," from the computer and get excited. "That for me, Frank?"

Fr. Tom was one who took the time to email Chris, and Frank helped Chris respond by typing for him whatever he wanted to say. When done, Chris would say, "Send it," and he knew the *send* button that Frank would have him hit. He would be happy with the emailing. There were many emails from family members and some Faith and Light parents, but Chris got especially excited when an email came from Fr. Tom.

Frank was thinking about adding a room onto the trailer, so that Chris could have an office of his own where he could have his computer, puzzle table, and storage space for his materials. They talked about this goal, and Chris wanted a good desk, and a place to hang his keys. As soon as they had moved into the trailer, Frank had filled a key ring for Chris and told him he was in charge of all the keys to the trailer, the shed, and anything else that required a key. They often sat, evenings, talking of this plan for an addition to the trailer. They decided to put off that project until Spring.

CHAPTER 5

Potato Soup and Sunflower Seeds

I had taken two days off from work specifically to spend some time with Chris and get him to his monthly Faith and Life meeting. The meetings provided his social life in the gathering of friends with special needs. Fr. Pat (who was the chaplain for the group), and Bill, the Director, led the program for our community named Faith, Family, and Friends. Although Frank and Chris lived quite a distance from where the meetings were held, Frank made sure Chris got to his meetings. Frank sometimes helped with the meetings, but sincerely believed Chris needed this time to be independent and on his own. In this particular week, I felt an unusually strong desire to spend some time with Chris and get him to the meeting.

I picked him up at noon after having a nice 45-minute drive up the Ute Pass on that warm September morning. The Aspen trees were at their golden autumn peak, glistening in the sunlight against the deep color of the evergreens. Colorado's blue sky was cloudless and I stopped by the pond while the local herd of deer crossed the road. Opening my window, I turned up the radio so they could hear the music, and to watch their reaction. Most of them just continued slowly crossing but one stopped, turned, and seemed to be listening to the country song. That particular deer suddenly jumped, as if to acknowledge the beat of the song, and went bouncing forward over the shrubbery across from the pond. The others immediately followed and I continued on my way, uplifted by the gifts of nature on that beautiful morning.

I arrived at the trailer to see Chris, next to his overnight bag, waiting and waving to me on the deck. He was ready to leave but Frank wanted to show me a website he was designing, and he called me inside. He had made lunch for us and invited us outside to enjoy it at the picnic table. Chris gulped his sandwich and salad down quickly as Frank and I talked. We both knew how anxious Chris was to leave as he always was whenever he was going somewhere, but I also wanted to spend a little time with Frank. Back inside, I sat for a while as he explained his computer work.

"Badda Bing! Badda Boom!" he exclaimed as the screen seemed to suddenly and magically fill up with the animated website. I was very impressed with his work and fascinated in the way he explained it all to me. "See? Watch this!" He was having fun showing me the progress he had made and the ways he planned to complete the site. He was taking online computer courses and wanted me to see what he was experimenting with. Chris patiently waited and watched until we were finished, but he laughed as always at Frank's repeated expression, "Badda Bing! Badda Boom!" Once I stood up and placed my coffee mug in the sink Chris hurried to the car, calling, "Bye Harry," behind him. "Harry", that pet name my husband had started with Chris, then all his sons; and that they continued with each other, and even called my brother, their Uncle Fred, "Harry" as an actual term of sentiment. Frank came outside to quickly review the imaginary checklist to be sure Chris had everything with him he needed. "I got it. I got it," Chris impatiently responded as I got into the car and we buckled our seatbelts. As we drove slowly up the long dirt driveway, Chris leaned out the window, and waved to Frank. "Bye, Harry!" he shouted. Frank smiled, gave a wave, and called back, "Bye, Harry."

Chris began asking me, one by one, about each of his siblings and their families and how they were doing. He seemed especially focused on his youngest sister's baby boy, Ben. "You will see your grandson, Ben, this weekend huh?" he asked. I explained I would not be seeing him that weekend, but told him about the dried sunflowers they had left at my apartment for him. There were two huge sunflowers waiting for him to remove the seeds for feeding the birds. That got him quite excited and anxious to reach my place. I told him we would put down newspapers before he started working on the sunflowers. Once we parked and walked through the breezeway to my apartment, he was breathing fast, I supposed, from excitement. He rushed through the door, right to the sunflowers. Then he laughingly stated, "Oh! They're BIG!"

He wanted to sit on the floor to pick the seeds from the sunflowers rather than at the table, so we put the newspapers down and he sat his tall body down to begin the work. I was baking cookies for him to take to his meeting while he was busy with the sunflowers, and gradually I heard him over the sound of the tv, groaning as he picked the seeds with his long fingers. I asked him if his hands hurt from the work, and he assured me, "No, Mom. No." The sounds of his groans grew louder, so I offered to help. I had trouble even getting a seed at a time out, so I got him a screwdriver. He attempted using the screwdriver but quickly put it down and went back to picking the seeds with his fingers. I made him a snack so he would take a break after a while, but he quickly gulped it down and told me he had to finish the seeds. "The birds will like the seeds!" he happily said. I asked him if it hurt to pick the seeds, and he said it didn't. However, as the afternoon passed, his groans continued as he bent over the sunflowers, picking away. I finally suggested that he had enough seeds for now and could let Frank help him the next day.

"No, Mom. I want to do it, " he told me as he continued for two hours of picking. I kept offering reasons for him to take a break or stop completely, as he seemed in pain, but he refused. Finally, late afternoon, I was very relieved when he stood up and smiling broadly, told me he was finished. He twisted and stretched his back as he said, "That was a lot of work!" We packed up the seeds as I noticed not even one seed was left in the dried up flowers, and together we cleaned up the newspapers. He wanted to then shower and get ready for his meeting.

Meanwhile, I was enjoying making potato soup for supper, something Chris had always liked. I turned off the tv and quietly set the table for the two of us. I wanted him to feel special, so I used pretty placemats and matching plates and soup bowls decorated with daisies. When he came out of the bathroom, all ready in his Faith & Light t-shirt and favorite black pants, he sat down at the table to wait for supper. "Hey, Mom," he suddenly said, "it says 'seed' here." He was pointing to the logo on the plate beneath the daisies, which read, "Sunshine Seed Co." We both smiled at what I hadn't even noticed about the table setting for our supper.

I served the soup, along with Irish Soda Bread I had made, and sat down opposite Chris. We prayed Grace and enjoyed a wonderful time together, talking about his friends at Faith and Light, about the family, and about plans for his next birthday, November 23rd. Since he and his brother Paul shared birthdays on that day, Paul had asked Chris what he would like him to cook for his birthday and he had told him spaghetti and meatballs. He told me they might have 2 birthday cakes too. Paul had always made Chris's birthday more important than his own, even as a child..

After our supper we left with the freshly baked cookies for the meeting. I dropped him off at the Parish Center for the meeting, where his long-time friend, John, came out and gave him a big hug and welcomed him as always. John is another parent and he and his wife, Diane, for many years had been the coordinators of the Faith and Light group. It was John who made Chris comfortable when he first began attending the meetings 15 years before.

Chris agreed to call me if he needed a ride home, and. he did call me after an hour to tell me his friend, Bill, would drive him home. Bill was retired and lived not too far from me, and he was at the time the Coordinator for the group.

I expected Chris home about 9:15 p.m. as usual but began dozing on my reclining chair about 9:30, waiting for him. It was almost 10:00 p.m. when I heard his hard knock on the door. I jumped up, and upon opening the door, saw Chris standing there staring into space as if in a trance. I said, "Chris?" He acted startled and then focused his eyes on me and seemed surprised as he said, "Oh, hi Mom." He came in and handed me a blue cardboard with a a bird printed on it, waiting to be colored. He also handed me a package of paint brushes with a set of water paints. "It's for Rosemary to paint for Ben!" he said excitedly. "I signed my name on it for Ben!" he added. "Will you give it to Rosemary for my nephew this weekend?" he asked. I reminded him I wouldn't see them this weekend but would give it to my daughter, Rose, the next time I saw her. We talked about how happy little Ben would be to have this bird from his Uncle Chris and painted by his mother.

Next he handed me a long white cloth stole where he had signed his name, Chris Montesano, and had drawn a very colorful rainbow. "I'm making it for you, Mom!" he said as he handed it to me. "Will you keep it here for my next meeting?" I agreed to keep it for him. I remembered another stole he had once made where he had written "We are happy." His gifts were always so sweet and meaningful.

Then we both agreed we were tired, and Chris was preparing his sleeping bag as I went to my bedroom and fell asleep feeling very good about him, and thanking God for a special day.

CHAPTER 6

Biscuits, Gravy, and the Blue Heron

I awoke early the next morning and was saying my prayers when Chris woke up. I greeted him, standing there shivering in his pajamas in my apartment living room where he had slept in his sleeping bag. Chris always smiled upon waking and was anxious to start the day with a meaningful, "Good Morning!" I opened the blinds and was shocked at the deep fog outside. I turned the heat on to take the chill off my small apartment. As Chris went to shower I began making his breakfast of biscuits and gravy. As I set the table and began putting breakfast out, he soon appeared all dressed and ready to go. "Mom, what time we leaving?" I was driving him home in the morning because he was very anxious to get the sunflower seeds to the birds. We decided we would leave about 10:00 a.m. Knowing the exact time for leaving calmed him as he had always been one who became anxious needing to know dates and times for whatever he was doing.

He and I ate breakfast and enjoyed a good morning conversation. He asked for a second cup of coffee and he talked a lot about little nephew Ben, and we looked at the bird picture for him. We planned how I would drive him home, and then Frank and I had an appointment in town. I encouraged Chris to ride with us, but he didn't want to. He said he would just stay home once he got there. He ate 2 helpings of the biscuits and gravy and we enjoyed our mugs of coffee together. He told me all about the Faith and Light meeting on the previous night. What a relaxing morning it was! We weren't rushed at all, and even watched the morning news together and talked about it. It was an exceptionally peaceful time for us, reflecting and conversing. As 10:00a.m. approached we left the apartment with Chris reminding me to give the bird picture and the paintbrushes to his sister, Rosemary, to paint for her small son, Ben. Once in the car he told me, "You will keep the stole, right Mom?" I assured him I would keep the white stole he had started making with his name autographed on it. He had also drawn a rainbow on it. "Maybe we'll see a rainbow like my stole, today," he suggested. He recalled the beautiful bright rainbow we had recently seen directly over their trailer home. Frank had put a picture of it on our family website.

We drove through the worsening fog up the mountain pass towards Chris's home in the woods. I had to put the heater on due to the fog and drizzle of the cold September morning. I drove slowly due to the weather, as Chris talked about little Ben and about feeding the sunflower seeds to the birds. Three different times, he asked the same question, "Will you see Ben this weekend?" Each time I told him that I would not be seeing my little grandson this weekend because his parents had other things to do. He smiled and said, "You love Ben, right Mom?" I assured him I did and we talked about the cute things little Ben did at the time. Twice during the ride, Chris leaned way forward staring, and I thought he was trying to see through the fog.

As we left the highway and began driving on the dirt road leading to the trailer, the fog began lifting, and we talked about that. We were passing the pond where we usually saw ducks in the summer and springtime, when we both were startled by a huge blue bird seemingly standing at attention, tall and proud, by the road as we passed him. Chris got excited and said, "Mom! Mom! That's the bird Frank always sees here!" There was the bird I had never seen before on my many trips to and from the trailer. There was the "big blue bird." It seemed so strange how straight and tall he stood and remained as we drove closely past him. He seemed frozen in the standing position, similar to a soldier standing at attention as we passed. I kept looking in the rear view mirror to see if the large bird moved as we drove away, but it remained "at attention." That seemed strange to me and caused me to keep looking in the rear-view-mirror waiting for some motion which I never did witness.

As we drove down the driveway to the trailer, we saw Frank on the deck drinking a mug of coffee. Chris turned to me and again asked, "Mom, you going to see Ben this weekend? You love him, huh?" I again reminded him that Rose had a busy weekend planned, and I would not see Ben. Once I parked, Chris excitedly burst from the car to show Frank all the sunflower seeds he had for the birds. Frank was happy about that. Chris went to get his ladder to begin filling the bird feeders, but Frank wanted him to first tell him about the Faith and Light meeting. Chris hurriedly told Frank about who had been at the meeting, what snacks they had, "the cookies Mom made", what they talked about, etc. Then Frank said, "Well, go feed the birds and I'll shut down my computer. We have to drive downtown to our appointment. You're coming right?"

Chris told Frank he didn't want to go, that he would stay and watch the trailer while we were gone. Frank tried to persuade him, because he had always wanted to ride along and not be home alone, but Chris would not give in. He wanted to stay home and feed the birds. We told him we would bring home some good food for lunch, and he liked that idea. While Frank was finishing some work on the computer and then shutting it down, I watched Chris climb the ladder to fill the first bird feeder, all the time calling out to the birds and telling them he had sunflower seeds for them from his sister, Rosemary, and her husband. He was happy, especially as the fog was lifting and the sun was starting to shine through. He called to me that the sun was out! Then he called out to the birds, telling them the same news: "Hey Birds, the sun is out! Come get sunflower seeds!"

As Frank and I started driving up the driveway, he noticed the front porch light was still on from the night before. After blowing the car horn to get Chris's attention, Frank leaned out the window and pointed to the light. Chris hurried over and turned the light off and began walking quickly back around the trailer to resume feeding the birds. He suddenly stopped, turned, smiled broadly, and waved to us. "Bye, Mom." I waved.

"Bye, Harry." Frank laughed and shouted back, "Bye, Harry." We waved and drove off.

I was telling Frank what a nice, special visit I had with Chris; and how glad I was that I had taken the two days off to spend time with him. I talked about how good it felt to cook a few meals for him. Frank suddenly interrupted me as we were passing the pond,

"Whoa! Mom! Look!" Out from the bushes burst the huge blue bird Chris and I had seen on our way to the trailer. I quickly stopped the car.

"It's the Blue Heron I always tell you about! Beautiful, huh?"

It certainly was a beautiful scene! The Heron's wings spread very wide as it flew gracefully, majestically, upward away from us toward the East, towards the huge ball of sun now shining brightly over the pond. The blueness of the bird was brilliant in the sunlight. Frank wished he had his camera with him, but was happy I had finally seen the bird he had often told me about. It was certainly a "Kodak moment." It left us in silence as we continued our drive. It had actually taken our breath away. I don't think I will ever forget that breath-taking scene.

We finished our appointment, and stopped at the deli on our way home. Frank came out smiling about buying the swiss cheese we all liked and some ham, chips, and dip. It would be a good lunch for the 3 of us. When we got to the trailer, however, Chris wasn't there. We looked around the yard, called out to him, and decided he probably had gone to visit one of the neighbors as he often did.

I needed to get going so Frank made me a sandwich. It was delicious, and I enjoyed it while Frank commented that he was surprised Chris had left when he knew we were bringing back good treats for lunch.. Finally I decided to leave, and Frank was getting back to his work on the computer. I commented to Frank about how very peaceful it felt there.

He said, "Yeah, nice and quiet here in the woods. Sometimes all we hear is the sound of the birds."

As I was getting into the car, he assured me, "Don't worry about Chris, Mom. He always comes back." Then I slowly drove away. Going back down the mountain pass I was thanking God for the nice time I had spent with Chris, and for the time off from work to enjoy him..

When I got home, about 1:30 p.m., I turned on my computer and discovered a new email from Frank, saying that he had found Chris napping in his bed.

About 3:30 p.m. there was knocking on my door. When I opened it, my daughter, Rosemary, was standing there with tears streaming down her face. "Oh, Mom. Oh, Mom," was all she could say at first. We were hugging in my apartment as she sobbed. Then she blurted out, "Mom, it's Chris." She could hardly talk through her sobs. "Mom, Chris is dead."

I froze. NO! Oh, God! No! Not this. My Chris could not be gone. No! No!

I sank into a chair, feeling weak, and asked, "What happened?" Rose began tearfully telling me that she received a voice mail message from Frank, while she was at work as a teacher in a middle school. Frank had sounded upset and hard to understand leaving the message. When she called her husband, who was at home with little Ben, he told her Frank had called saying he had found Chris dead in his bed. Just then she got another call from her sister, Donna, who asked her to drive to my home and give me the news. That was all she knew when she arrived at my door.

Rose offered to call the church office and let our priests know. It was a short time afterward when Fr. Pat arrived at my apartment to pray with us and talk with us. All I could say was, "He fed the birds and went to sleep." Then Fr. Tom arrived to be with us. My children began slowly arriving, overcome with shock and tears. No one knew all the details as we all waited for Frank to arrive with his brothers, Mike and Paul. They told me that Frank had thought Chris was quietly napping, and finally went to his room to rouse him for lunch. He noticed Chris had taken the time to put aside his glasses and hearing aid, and to pull the blanket over himself, and was on his side facing away from the doorway where Frank had originally looked in.

Unable to rouse Chris and upon finding him motionless, Frank frantically began CPR, unwilling to believe his brother was gone. He dialed 911 for help, and kept trying to revive his brother. It was twenty minutes before the firemen and police arrived, and Frank had to accept the truth. He had phoned his brothers and sisters, including Paul and Mike who rushed there from their jobs, in time to witness their brother Chris's body being removed from the trailer and taken to the nearby morgue. They wept with Frank and comforted him and then drove to my apartment.

My children were silent in my living room except for sniffling and soft moans. When they talked, it was about regrets of not spending more time with Chris, of the plans they had held for the future of getting together with him, of what they had planned to give him for his next birthday. After a while some of them left to go to my daughter, Donna's house. Rosemary, her husband, and little Ben stayed with me. They cried about Ben not getting to know his Uncle Chris. They wished they had brought Ben more often to visit Chris. I went to my bedroom and got the bird picture, paints, and paintbrushes Chris has asked me to give to Rose for Ben. The gift just broke them down more. They couldn't believe that Chris had so thought of little Ben on his last days. Then I told them how he kept asking me about seeing Ben on the weekend, and we all realized I certainly would be spending the weekend with him every day now as we moved toward planning a funeral mass. Rose asked me to keep the bird picture until she was strong enough to take it. She asked me to save it for Ben.

At supper time, everyone returned to my apartment bringing food, and we all shared a meal together. We began to share some memories in that early time of his passing, and even to laugh a bit through our tears about the one who had held us together as a family and gave us laughter so often. I kept repeating myself, "He fed the birds and went to sleep."

Donna told me how, at her house, they had been looking through the second book I wrote about Chris. They were reading aloud what he had said about each of them, and they realized he had spent his life helping everyone and being happy and cheerful doing it. They wept and expressed some guilt about having him help with laundry, snow shoveling, moving furniture, cleaning, etc. But they all agreed as a group that it really had brought him happiness and a feeling of worth. Together now we even laughed tearfully at how he probably saw through us more than we had known.

Listening to them I realized I had given birth to a true servant of God. I had also given birth to these wonderful brothers and sisters of his who always appreciated him and included him. I felt overwhelmingly blessed in that moment. I recalled the time when my husband and I were told of Chris's diagnosis and warned not to have more children. In that moment we had decided to go ahead with our plan for a large family because we thought it might give our special little boy more helpers through life. They had always been his best friends. Tears welled in me now, in the intense pain of looking at all of them....each of them.... in their new sorrow.

CHAPTER 7
The Day After

It was 5:00 a.m., and I sat in the darkness in disbelief. It was my morning prayer time. I slowly picked up the prayer I had written many years before, to pray as I always did. It felt very heavy though it was simply a piece of paper. In routine fashion I began praying the prayer until I was stunned to see one of the lines I had written long ago appearing brighter and larger than all the others: "When our time comes, please allow each of us the gift of a peaceful death."

The pain in my heart felt more piercing as I reread that request to God. I realized that I had been reading that prayer I had written for many, many years, sometimes simply routinely without much thought to that line. I began to cry in my gratitude for Chris's extraordinary peaceful death the day before, although it was hard to be grateful in the moment. I sat there in the dark, reasoning that if a mother had to lose her child, one of the few comforts could be a peaceful death. It could not have been more peaceful for him than to simply lie down and be gone. As I sat there thinking about it, I really did feel consoled by the fact that Chris had died peacefully, and hoped it would help my children and their families in their grieving. My heavy heart sighed as the phone's ringing interrupted my thoughts. The children started calling, and we began our day of discussing funeral plans.

It was hard for me to look at each of my grown children, utterly devastated on that day; and it seemed hard for them to look at each other. They already looked pale and drained from the shock and exhaustion of the past 24 hours.

"Why didn't I cut his hair like he asked me last week?" My daughter questioned aloud. Her voice choked as she repeated, "Why didn't I just cut his hair?" She could hardly talk, "I told him I was too busy." She put her head down crying. Another daughter sat blankly staring at me, and finally said she had planned on calling him, planned on spending more time with him, planned on taking him clothes shopping again......soon.

There were moments like that throughout the day with my children when they either shared their thoughts or cried quietly. We had a conversation about the guilt that always seems to arise at the time of death of a loved one. Always we feel we should have done more for them. So we tried to talk more about how he made us laugh, and what he would say to us now. We were able to share some genuine fun-filled memories we had enjoyed with Chris, and we ate together and appreciated all we had been blessed with by his life...laughing and crying through our flowing tears. I found it comforting to say, "He just fed the birds and went to sleep."

The coroner called on that day and asked if I would like an autopsy done. I wanted one for my children especially, to answer their questions about this sudden quiet death of their brother. The coroner agreed it might help us to understand the untimely death.

My sister called from New York to tell me, "I'll never forget that sweet quiet child. Let me buy the flowers to cover his casket." Her comment reminded me of that sweet quiet child who had lived on in those 46 years....always a child.

My kids told me how they had stayed up late together the night before, going over the book I had written about Chris, where I had interviewed him about his feelings regarding each of them as well as other family members and friends. As they had read the comments regarding themselves, they were astounded at how grateful he had always been for the simple opportunities he had experienced just talking with them or helping them, always appreciative for them in his life. He had talked so enthusiastically to me about his siblings:

"He helps me. He likes to talk about things with me and we have good talks. He likes to plan things with me."

"He lets me help him with the laundry. He lets me help him shovel snow, and one night he told me he loves me, and we drank Pepsi together."

"He takes me to the store sometimes. He lets me sleep at his house and clean his yard and rake the leaves. I know he cares about me."

"She bought me lots of beads so I can make her a necklace. I hope she likes what I make for her."

"When I washed her dishes, she said I did a good job. Sometimes I help her fold laundry and she said I do that good too."

"She helps me a lot and takes me to her house. I remember when I helped her move into her new house."

On that day after he left us, we experienced the summing up of his life in his own words. It was devastating to watch my grown children entering this grief. It already felt different than the grief-stricken children I had once faced when their father died. The depth of sorrow was similar now, but their reactions were not the same, and the memories of their father's death resurfaced. One who had been 10 years old when his father died, now got into his car and drove away across several states, wanting only to get away from what he didn't want to go through again. It was a few days before he returned for the funeral but did not feel strong enough to attend another viewing. I understood. Each of my grown children would face darkness and death in their own way, just as they had done as children, and I would honor their individual coping. I would try to be supportive to each one in different ways they would need. Now there were many nieces and nephews crying for their Uncle Chris, and they too needed our support. There were even several great-nieces and nephews sharing in this sorrow.

It was shattering for me to look at all of them. Where would I find the strength to get through these days? We all agreed that we believed Chris was now relieved from pain and suffering, and would be happy and whole with The Lord. That thought consoled us, but our tears flowed non-stop. Jimmy was so grateful for the recent weekend he had with Chris. He had invited Chris to spend the weekend with him and his children, and Chris had fun teaching the youngest boy, Joey, how to fold laundry properly. He took a walk with his niece through their small town, and the two adult brothers, Jimmy and Chris, enjoyed meals and conversation together. Jimmy now kept repeating, "Thank God we had our weekend with him! Thank God for that!"

Each person who called that day had a memory to share about Chris. Each of their memories pierced my heart as I relayed them to my children and watched their reactions. So many people commented on how Chris had always greeted them with a smile and a cheerful welcome. Many shared their disbelief how he had remembered their middle names and even their birthdays. He had made them feel special. Each caller had a story to tell about an experience with Chris. One of his cousins called to tell me how she had always loved him, loved playing with him as a child, and had named her own son, Christopher, for him. Many of Chris's cousins called to say he had been their favorite cousin. One by one, we agreed that he was relieved of pain and suffering now, relieved of his handicaps, relieved of his weaknesses. Now he could hear and see perfectly, and enjoy Heaven; and those thoughts helped all of us, especially the youngest children.

My daughter, Patti, gave me a small golden angel-face ornament which I hung over the puzzle Chris had made for me. Paul said he could never celebrate his birthday again and wrote a poem:

"A great man has passed

A great Brother is gone

The world has lost one brave and strong

Always a smile

Always a grin

Our special brother Chris lived without sin

The gift of Chris

Was for us all

I hear his laugh whenever I fall

Ha ha ha...you ok Paul?

A great man has passed

A great brother is gone

A great brother to me and friend to all

I already miss those special calls

This special guy

This blessed man

Our great friend Chris with all those cans

I thank God and Heaven above

I thank God for all His love".....Love, Paul

By late afternoon my children were deciding on the evening meal we would have together, each chipping in whatever money they could, so that we would have our supper together.

Somehow, we got through that first day following their brother's death. We prayed together our Grace Before Meals, and ate enough to sustain us, encouraging each other that we had to eat and keep our strength.

We formed our plans to meet at the church the following day to discuss funeral plans with the priest and liturgist. We all agreed that we wanted the service to genuinely be a tribute to Chris's life. We would be thinking of ideas to bring to the next day's meeting. I was in touch with the one son who had driven away, and he assured me that he would be present for the service we planned; he and his children would be there. My children left, except my oldest son, Frank....Chris's caretaker for so many years stayed with me. We had all managed to help each other through the first day.

CHAPTER 8
Clothespin Crucifix

Fr. Tom and Sue, the parish liturgist led us through the planning of Chris's funeral mass. We exchanged ideas for readings and agreed the songs should be Chris's favorites. It was hard to believe we were planning the celebration of Chris's life already. He was only 46. The look of grief had returned to my children's eyes again, as Chris's death brought back the memories of their father's sudden death. The weight of missing their brother already hung over the room. There was no feeling of enthusiasm for the choices we made for the liturgy, only agreement, only unity. Mike had stayed up late the night before, going through scripture, and had chosen readings as he sought comfort in his Bible. Fr. Tom had me stand and read those Bible readings as well as some he himself was suggesting. I was surprised at the strength I felt as I stood reading those scripture selections to my children. How could I feel strong at such a time?

The weekend came and I realized Ben had been with us every day, and now on the weekend. He was a happy one-year-old, lifting our spirits. Everyone was deciding what to wear for the funeral mass, and my daughter Rose, chose a purple outfit for me. My daughters and daughters-in-law agreed we would wear the bead necklaces Chris had made for each of us.

The physician who had performed the autopsy called to inform me that Chris had died from a ruptured weakness in his aorta. A feeling of fatigue would have overcome him, causing him to want to sleep. Frank had asked the doctor if we could have done anything to prevent Chris's death, and the response that he got was, "No, this weakness was hereditary and was just never detected during his lifetime. It happened quickly and without pain or suffering. He actually just lay down and went to sleep." It was true: He fed the birds and went to sleep. What comfort!

Then came Monday evening for the wake, the viewing. Chris would be wearing his favorite tan sweater when we went to pray together and see him for the last time. My daughter, Donna, arrived early at the funeral home with her husband and children. As she reached the door, the funeral director approached her and said, "I'm sorry, but your brother is stuck in traffic."

"Which brother?" Donna asked in confusion. "Your brother, Chris," the director spoke in a whispered voice. "We'll be a bit late starting because we have to wait for him to arrive."

As Donna stood there trying to make sense of the conversation, the man in the black suit continued in a hushed professional tone, "There was a traffic jam on the highway as your brother was being transported from the autopsy procedure at the hospital. The funeral car should be here soon, and we'll get started."

As we all gathered, we waited outside the funeral home explaining to everyone that Chris wasn't ready yet.

Finally, the door opened and we were invited to enter. Those of the family who expressed a desire not to see him in the casket agreed to sit in the back of the room. Some edged forward slowly for one last look at their brother, uncle, great-uncle, brother-in-law, cousin, nephew, neighbor, acquaintance, friend. I walked slowly towards my son, and then felt relieved to see him looking so natural and peaceful lying there. I noticed the floral blanket my sister has sent to cover the casket of "the sweet quiet boy" she was remembering. I sat down opposite the casket as everyone slowly came forward to pay respects, and then sit down. Two of my teenage granddaughters sat down beside me and that was comforting. The room was full but quiet when my daughter, Rosemary, from behind me let out a sob. As I turned to look at her I saw some parents coming into the room with Chris's handicapped friends. Rosemary was watching them. The parents were helping the young people forward to pay their last respects to their good friend, Chris, and were being brave and solemn with the support of their parents. Stephen's father was leading, guiding Stephen who always wore a helmut to prevent injury from falling in his reoccurring seizures. They all stood or knelt next to Chris for a few minutes and then went to sit as a group before Fr. Tom announced we would pray the Rosary together. It was very hard to hear crying during the Rosary, but it was good to pray together. I knew we were all remembering our family Rosaries when they were children, with Chris struggling to get the words right. I was trying to be strong for everyone, trying to help them all through this, asking God constantly to fill me with strength and courage. Each time I prayed that request in my heart I was filled with peace and calm from the top of my head down to my toes.

My inner thoughts were of wonder about this happening. How could Chris be gone? I had always been concerned about

Chris's care after I was gone. With the children in agreement, I had a Will made up outlining his care going from one child to the other through the years after I would die. So many times I had discussed with other parents our fears for these handicapped children of ours after we were gone. Who would take care of them? Now here I was looking at my child in a casket.

That night, alone in my room the tears flowed freely....so devastated that my Chris was gone. It was as though his face kept appearing, his voice kept sounding, his words, "Mom... Mom" kept overwhelming me in the darkness. I went to a drawer and found my favorite picture of him, when he was about 6 years old, and finally fell asleep with it in my hand. I kept waking up thinking I heard my child, Chris, calling me as a little boy. It was a very long night. At one point I got up and took out a Canadian magazine, "Our Family," January 1976 issue. In it I read the article I once had written to express the thoughts of my husband. I wrote what he expressed to me.. Now I read it with new meaning, almost 20 years later:

A FATHER'S PRAYER

Dear God, in a few days Chris will reach his sixteenth birthday. Thus far, you have given me the ability to understand and accept him as my retarded son, the knowledge to guide him, and the faith to believe in him. You gave me the strength to help him over many hurdles.

Now, I pray that you will grant Chris the same gifts; that you will help him to understand his handicaps and to accept himself. Let him find some sense of direction in his world of frustration.

Please give him the confidence to believe in himself. Above all, Lord, Chris will need a tremendous amount of courage as he faces this birthday with the same dreams held by most boys of his age.

Please guide me as I explain to him why he can't drive a car. He longs so much to do so.

Now that he has finished his schooling, he doesn't really understand why he can't go on to college with his brothers. Help me to show him his value without it.

He would like a job where he could earn money. Direct me, Father, to find such placement for him.

When he joins the conversations of his brothers and sisters as they talk of dating, marriage and raising families, I beg of you to ease him into the realization that he will not have such privileges. Perhaps you could show him, eventually, that being a "good uncle" will be enough.

He is beginning to notice small children staring and sometimes laughing at him. Lord, please keep up his great sense of humor and let him continue to laugh at his own mistakes.

He seems to be losing his enthusiasm for competing in games and sports. I hope that this is a loss of interest rather than a feeling of failure.

Chris is gradually realizing that he is different. Please let him see his difference is his greatness.

Dear Father in heaven, I stand in awe of this special son of mine, begging your assistance for him, while feeling your tremendous love for him. You have given me a difficult part in your work on this earth; but you have blessed me with its rewards.

I often wish that all of my children could love you in the simple and open way that Chris does. You have introduced me to famous people, doctors, teachers, bishops and cardinals through him. I have enjoyed the beautiful virtues he has drawn from his brothers and sisters. And you know, Lord, how many lives he has touched in his innocent way. I thank you.

I ask that you stay very close to my son, now, as he faces more hardships on his lonely road. And if your plan for Chris happens to be mainly to bring your love into this world, Father, please notice his success. Amen

****

Suddenly it was The Feast Day of St. Francis of Assisi, October 4th. It was the day we had chosen for Chris's funeral mass. I had gone to a local printer and had several copies printed of the Prayer of St. Francis to be available for everyone at the church. I assembled the gray cards in a box to carry them to the church. I bravely got dressed in my purple outfit, put on the colorful bead necklaces he had made for me, and went to church for my son's funeral service. I kept asking God to fill me with strength and courage for the day. It was to be a celebration of Chris's life, but I didn't feel at all like celebrating.

Arriving early, my children and I took our seats with their spouses, children, and grandchildren to celebrate Uncle Chris's life. They were all dressed in their "Sunday Best" but most were hardly smiling. Mike was wearing the suit he had bought the previous day at Good Will, the non-profit organization where Chris had once worked. Ben too was in his Sunday Best, and was smiling and waving at me. His mother, Rosemary, was weakly smiling at me through tear-filled eyes. As the church was filling, I was grateful and comforted to see so many friends of all of us arriving to join in the celebration of Chris Montesano's life.

My children and I were called to the doorway of the church as the closed casket was carried to the entrance by Chris's nephews. Fr. Tom began the Mass with the Sign of The Cross and prayerfully invited all to join in celebrating Chris's life. I felt as though I was dragging myself to the casket.

"Frank and Pat are now covering the casket with the white cloth that represents the white clothing Chris wore at his Baptism," (He was the only one of my children who had worn a beautiful long woolen white hooded Baptismal cape that my parents had purchased just for him.) Frank and I draped the coffin and made sure the cloth was even and straight. Then Fr. Tom announced that I would be placing a small crucifix on it. "A crucifix Chris had made with wooden clothespins at a Faith and Light meeting," Father explained. As I went to put the sweet little cross on the casket, I remembered Chris standing at my door full of excitement to tell me, "Mom! Look what I made for you!" I now felt tears rising and my throat ready to sob. Right then the organ music began, with the song we had chosen to bring Chris into the church for the last time: "He's Got The Whole World In His Hands." As we turned to begin the procession down the aisle, I was very surprised to hear my voice loud and clearly singing! I was filled with a feeling of happiness as I started walking and kept singing louder and louder and even smiling. I did not feel like crying at all! It was amazing! I sang all the way down the aisle to my seat, and we continued singing, "He's got the whole world in His hands," until everyone was in the church and the casket was in front of the alter at the large Paschal Candle. That tall candle is always used during Catholic funeral masses, to remind us of Easter and the Resurrection. Jesus had died and risen from the dead, and Chris had lived in that belief. The Paschal Candle looked bigger than ever to me as it seemed to stand looking down at Chris and the little clothespin crucifix.

At the end of the song, I turned to acknowledge the Faith and Light membership opposite us in the front rows of the church, as we had requested. There they were in their "Sunday Best," in their suits and ties and pretty dresses. Some of them had been friends to Chris for more than 15 years. Their voices had been loud and clear also, singing the song so familiar to them from their meetings. They were prepared to acknowledge the life of their friend.

Fr. Tom gave a wonderful homily that morning, which included his story about Chris always saying he prayed for Father's aching foot. "You know," Fr. Tom told us smilingly, "my foot actually feels better today." He said Chris's prayers had been valuable, and recalled Chris telling many people he prayed for them. After the homily, in some moments of silence, I looked at the Paschal Candle and thought about Chris's role in our lives; he had been our Easter Light for 46 years. During the time of sprinkling the casket and with the scent of incense around us, I realized that Chris was the one who held us together, who led us closer to God through his life of suffering. I slowly realized that my granddaughters were wearing the bead necklaces he had made for them. Then everyone in the church held the prayer cards I had made and we all prayed aloud together the prayer of St. Francis.

Lord, make me an instrument of Your peace; where there is hatred, let me sow love; where there is injury, pardon; where there is doubt, faith; where there is despair, hope; where there is darkness, light; and where there is sadness, joy. O Divine Master, grant that I may not so much seek to be consoled as to console; to be understood as to understand; to be loved, as to love; for it is in giving that we receive, it is in pardoning that we are pardoned, and it is in dying that we are born to eternal life.

I heard also that day the words repeated during every Catholic Funeral Mass, "Life has not ended but only changed." I truly believed that Chris's suffering was finished.

When it was time for the Offertory Procession, all the nieces and nephews went behind us and assembled. They slowly came down the aisle to the beautiful singing of Ave Maria by a local artist, each carrying a large sunflower which they put into a vase at the alter. Most of them had tears streaming down their faces as they came forward. They all understood the many meanings of the sunflowers for their Uncle Chris. They each had their own memories of him. Some of them were too young to understand the loss they were going to experience. Some of them were wearing the necklaces he had made for them. They were all dressed in their best clothes. I was thinking how Chris had been their good uncle always, how they had been the children of his life. I thought of "A Father's Prayer" that my husband and I had written: *"Perhaps you could show him, eventually, that being a 'good uncle' will be enough."*

I helped to distribute Communion and marveled at my own strength and courage in doing so. I was smiling at all those coming forward and they were trying to smile through their tears. My nephew Bobby, who had always been good and kind to Chris, came forward with his son and smiled very broadly at me and actually looked happy. He later told me our celebration taught him that this really and truly was a time to celebrate his cousin's life, and to remember his cousin, Chris, who had always been smiling, and to know he's happier now than he's ever been. "This is about what we believe in," he later said to me.

At the end of the mass we all sang the words of Chris's very favorite song, "Mine eyes have seen the glory of the coming of the Lord......." I could hear sobs from my children, and saw the pain on Jimmy's face, but we kept singing and then followed the casket out of the church, where he was placed into the funeral car to be taken for cremation. We went into the church hall to share a meal prepared by ladies of our parish. As the crowd came into the cafeteria to join us in a wonderful sympathy meal prepared by the ladies of the church, I found myself strong enough to be greeting each person and talking with them, thanking them for coming. I had some beautiful conversations with many that day. Frank had spent the past few days, receiving photographs from his siblings to put into a slide show which he now presented. What a beautiful slide show he had assembled from so many pictures taken during his brother's life! I, personally, found it difficult to look at him in the pictures, but our guests enjoyed them. Chris's handicapped friends visited with each of us. One young man told us, "I will be Chris's smile at Faith and Light meetings."

During the funeral mass, one of the parents had asked me to bring back the stole Chris had started for me so his friends could finish it. At the meal, his friends all asked me to be sure and bring the stole to them. It was so important to them that they complete what Chris had lovingly started for me. I assured them I would return it to them. It was Chris's handicapped friends who stayed 'til the very end and walked outside with us, wishing us well and assuring us they would never forget Chris.

It was all over and we went to my apartment mid-afternoon. My grandson, Ben, and his parents stayed with me. The rest of my family went to each other's homes and visited with each other and friends. After a light supper Ben and his parents left, and I folded up Chris's favorite black pants and put them at the foot of my bed. (They are still there. For some reason it feels right to refold those pants and put them at the foot of my bed each day.)

It was early when I thanked God for getting me through the day, and I fell asleep crying, holding that favorite picture of my sweet quiet boy at age 6, the same boy whose valuable life we had just celebrated.

CHAPTER 9

Gathering at the Cemetery

How would I get through each day, I wondered. Where would I find the strength? I resumed my desperate simple daily prayer of years before: "God, please fill me with the strength I need for today."

For several years I had been a proclaimer at our church, reading scripture to parishioners assembled for mass. I had committed to doing this on Monday mornings for our daily masses. I thought I would not be able to continue that ministry when Chris died, but decided to give it a try. I felt as though I was starting to hyperventilate the first Monday I walked up the steps to the lectern. I tried to take a deep breath before starting. It was hard to say the first word. I read the first sentence. Then I read the next sentence. As I read I realized I was feeling stronger and stronger as I read. Then I was feeling unusually comfortable and calm and breathing easier as I read. I got through it that first Monday, and the next Monday, and the next, etc. I finally realized that my greatest source of strength was coming on Monday mornings to carry me through the week. My source was the Word of God! I don't know why I'm so often surprised at the power of God, but I find it awesome each time I'm renewed and refreshed. I was reading the Word of God for the glory of God, and I was actually experiencing the glory of God while grieving! I felt the goodness of God while my heart ached!

At the time of the funeral the Director of the funeral home told me we would be able to visit Chris's grave site 2 days later as he was being cremated after the mass, and they needed the following day to take his cremains to the military cemetery to his father's grave site for burial. So on the following Sunday, a very beautiful Autumn day, we drove to the military cemetery where Chris's remains were buried with his father. We were quite solemn driving to the grave site, but then all of us seemed to be uplifted by being there. Frank took pictures of us and the grave site. We marveled among us how perfectly the ashes had been buried, without a trace of grass appearing to be moved at all. We finally said a prayer together and slowly walked away. On the drive home there were some tears, mostly silence, and some shared reflections. It was sad. It was final.

About one month later I went to the funeral home to give a payment towards the funeral services for Chris. The girl who accepted my payment said, "I believe your son's remains will be going up there this week."

Excuse me? What did she say? In my shock and confusion, I asked her, "What do you mean?"

She replied in a calm reassuring tone, "We're backed up on burials, and should be able to get your son's remains to the grave site this week. A shipment will be going up."

"What?" I was dumbstruck. "Where is he?" I finally asked in my disbelief.

"Oh, he is at a holding house."

"What do you mean?" I questioned.

She seemed surprised by my confusion, and responded, "He's at another funeral home where we store cremains until we're able to get them to cemeteries.

"I want him buried now," I insisted. "We were told he was being buried the day after the funeral."

She turned to leave the room as she told me, "I'm sorry. We've been so busy. I'll be right back."

A few minutes later she re-entered the room and assured me they would make a special trip the following day to deliver my son's ashes for burial. I thanked her and left in shock.

That evening, calling my children with this news, we ended up laughing at ourselves visiting the grave site and being so solemn while Chris was actually in storage on a shelf.

The following week I called to confirm with the funeral home that Chris's remains had been taken to the cemetery and were buried with his father. I was assured he was now resting there.

We returned to the burial site a month later and saw Chris's name engraved on the back of the tombstone bearing my husband's name, and believed his ashes were now there. There were signs of a recent disturbance of grass. We prayed in acknowledgment of Chris being buried there with his Dad. We left them to rest in peace as we went home to continue our grieving.

We were helped through our grieving by the many thoughts and reflections shared by friends and family in the days and weeks that followed:

"What a beautiful crowd of folks who love Chris came together at his wake and funeral service. You all picked the perfect songs, readings, and prayers. May Jesus continue to lift you and each of the family in comfort and care."

"What a life he led! I loved seeing the jigsaw puzzle at his memorial service. I'm a puzzle worker too....I'll think of Chris every time I start a new one!"

"All that ailed him and gave him pain is gone now and his soul is free to fly with his friends the birds...."

"He had a prosperous full life with many friends and peoples' lives he touched...."

"When I think of the love that Chris had for all of nature, I can only believe that he is now one with the very creator of all that he loved, and so much a part of it all that there is no room for anything that would keep him from fully living in the completeness of that creation with all of those special creatures that he loved so much."

"Chris always had the faith and wonder of a child, and now he can rest in the arms of Jesus."

"Frank, I will always remember the big grin he got whenever I would show up at the house that you and he lived in. It seemed that he always had a smile on his face, and a song in his heart! I will miss him dearly."

"We miss his loving presence and ready smile."

"Bless You for being Chris's best friend for all these years, Frank. We are glad He had a certain childlike kindness. You are your brother's keeper, so keep his love alive."

CHAPTER 10

The First Anniversary

I was widowed young and had been making decisions for my family for over 30 years. Sitting in my small apartment, looking out on Pikes Peak, I reflected on the past year of grieving the loss of Chris, and when making everyday decisions for him no longer existed. After having him at the center of our family for 46 years, I was having a hard time adjusting to life without him....without his early morning phone calls asking, "How are you today?" I missed his reminders of all the family birthdays, and his holding the youngest nieces and nephews or grand-nieces and grand-nephews at family gatherings. It would be very hard to be without his child-like excitement every Christmas Eve. My heart longed for the happiness that had surrounded him living in the mountains, and for the sight of him on his porch waving and welcoming me as I drove down the driveway to the trailer. It was almost unbearable to see his friends without him, and to look at the photographs which people had given me throughout the year... of Chris with their families or at Faith and Light events. The reminders were there every day: his favorite foods, birthdays, holidays, the roads he had walked, the buses he had ridden, the places where he had worked, the shops where we had taken him, and in church. There were sudden moments of tears, such as the day I was in the grocery store choosing ice cream. When my eyes saw the chocolate ice cream, the tears flowed with restraint impossible. There I was in the grocery store, of all places, crying. That had been his favorite flavor. It was hard to have the memories. It was hard to accept the emptiness.

Now, I thought, how would we celebrate the first anniversary of his death? As Catholics, the traditional ritual would be a mass in Chris's memory on the date of his death. With such a large family it had become difficult to get all of us in one place at one time, so we decided we would each attend mass in our own parishes, quietly, at a time of each one's choosing and desire. Grief is such a personal experience, and sets its own timing and trials for each individual. For some members of our family, grieving was just beginning a year later; while others were deeply submerged in its difficult journey. The only decision we were able to agree on was that we needed to do something on September 28th to help all of us as we struggled with this great loss, especially for the very youngest family members who were so missing their Uncle Chris. We agreed that we all needed to be together to somehow celebrate Chris's life again. We weren't sure how to do that.

About a week before the 1st anniversary of Chris's passing, the Faith and Light group held their meeting and invited me to attend. I thought it would be hard to sit with Chris's special friends, but felt honored that they wanted me to be with them to remember their buddy, Chris. What an uplifting and strengthening evening it was! I sat with the members, all assembled in a circle as they each recalled their relationship with Chris. Sometimes they were funny, sometimes they were sad and tearful, but each memory was very touching. Fr. Pat read the day's gospel and gave a beautiful homily which included ways to remember those who have left us. He had everyone participate in the discussion about the readings and homily. Then we all prayed together for Chris and his family, and for ourselves in our grieving. There was such enthusiasm about celebrating Chris, and such simple sincerity in sharing feelings of missing him. We shared wonderful refreshments, and the members kept hugging me and telling me how much they missed Chris.

I was presented with the stole that Chris had started making for me, with his signature and the rainbow. Now it was filled with the beautiful remembrances of the individuals he had met with for more than 15 years. There, on the stole, were the items and notes these special adults had wanted for Chris: the Faith, Family, and Friends of Colorado Springs, CO membership pin which he had worn at meetings; a cross; a bird; the word Peace; a heart which says "Chris, You are unique and I love you". a pretty card with the Faith and Light logo and the words, "Happy the peacemakers-because they shall be called Sons of God;" and another little rainbow colored with crayons. Fr. Pat blessed the stole and placed it on me, and I wore it throughout the meeting and was blessed by it. I believe these friends of Chris understood my appreciation and gratitude for all they had done. To close the meeting everyone excitedly went outside to let white balloons go up into the evening sky for Chris. It was a beautiful star-lit Colorado night and the balloons were very visible at they floated away "towards Chris". There were smiles on all the sweet faces looking upward.

As I slowly drove home, tears flowed from being so overwhelmed with love and care from Chris's beautiful friends in their own grief. They had proudly showed me the empty chair they had placed in their circle at every meeting since Chris had left, " to represent his big smile".

The next morning, as I reflected on the very special Faith and Light meeting, my thoughts returned to wondering how our family would get together and spend the actual first anniversary coming soon: September 28th.

Some of us planned to drive to the cemetery for a visit at the graves of Chris and my husband, to bring flowers, and then share a picnic at the pond nearby. Most of us planned to do this, but some felt they were not ready emotionally. Those of us who would go planned to drive the 70 miles on the Sunday following the September 28th anniversary, which would be October 1st.

During September I went to the doctor for a routine physical. She prescribed a stress test as part of the exam, simply because I had never had one, and so it was scheduled for late-September. On the day of the exam I was busy with several work projects and errands and almost missed the test, arriving late and offering to reschedule. I was preparing for a plane trip to upstate New York to visit my aunts and uncles. I would be leaving on October 5th. I was too busy to be concerned about this test and offered to take it in late October after I returned from my trip. The medical staff scurried around and decided they could squeeze me in between other appointments. I reluctantly went to the waiting room for the procedure. I felt impatient waiting to be tested because I needed to prepare for my trip and felt no need for this. Finally, I was led to the stress test room and underwent an ultrasound procedure before getting on the treadmill. I immediately became short of breath while walking on the treadmill, and the technician asked how I felt. I explained, breathlessly, that I had been asthmatic all my life and that's why I was breathing heavily.

"Well, my chest feels tight, as when I'm having an asthma attack," I told him, as he brought the treadmill to a stop..

"It is not asthma," the technician responded. "It appears you might have a serious blockage, possibly as much as 70%." He told me we needed to go right away to see the cardiologist, and he escorted me through the building to the office of the heart specialist.

After examining the stress test report, and reviewing the films, the cardiologist told me I needed to schedule an angiogram to determine the seriousness of the blockage and the possibility of my need for a stent or possible surgery. *What?* I told him I never had any symptoms other than occasional shortness of breath which I attributed to asthma. I explained that I was planning to leave on a trip to New York on October

5th, and he told me there was no way I could travel with this blockage in my artery. I was alarmed! Miss my trip? No! It might be the last time I would see my aging aunts and uncles. I needed to go!

On September 26th I drove to the hospital for the angiogram. My daughters, Patti and Rosemary, accompanied me so I could have a ride home after the procedure, which required some sedation. I reminded the doctor, as we prepared to begin the angiogram, that I had plans to fly to New York in 1 week. He assured me I would probably be able to travel by then.

"There's no way you could go without having this procedure first," he assured me. "You will be able to go to New York in one week as long as everything goes as planned. If the angiogram shows you'll need bypass surgery, then you will not be able to travel."

On the morning of the angiogram the nurse asked me if I preferred to be awake or asleep during the procedure, and I chose to sleep. Very quickly I was asleep. When I woke up, I was looking into the face of my very concerned physician, who handed me copies of my films. "I did not install a stent because I discovered you have a much more serious blockage, more like 90%, and I need to order a special drug-coated stent for you."

He suggested I stay in the hospital for 2 days until he got

the stent. I agreed, and he began admission paperwork. "I don't know how you haven't had pain and symptoms with the degree of blockage you have in your artery," he said. Then he smiled, told me to rest, and assured me, "You will be able to fly to New York as planned following the stent procedure."

Late that afternoon, the attending nurse told me the doctor was able to get the stent already and had the procedure scheduled for the following day, September 28th.

Oh, no!

That was the anniversary of Chris's death.

I thought of my children and how difficult this would be for them. That evening Fr. Pat, came to visit and gave me the Anointing of The Sick. He then left me with the assurance that I was in God's hands. As I was falling asleep I thought about my children and the courage being required of them on the following day. I fell asleep praying for them, after asking Chris to pray for us.

****

"Frank!"

Early on the morning of September 28th, my oldest son was standing in the doorway of my hospital room, smiling as

I awoke. What a great surprise from the son who had been Chris's care giver for so many years. He had sold the mountain trailer and moved to a nice apartment in Denver where he was working his way through the college classes he needed to complete towards a degree in internet technology. Here he was in the hospital early on the first anniversary of Chris's death. He drank coffee while I fasted in preparation for the stent procedure. A nun arrived and offered us Communion, and Frank and I shared the only host she had brought with her, on the morning of the special day. She prayed a beautiful prayer and left us to visit and wait as some of my other children arrived to spend the morning with me. We were a bit concerned about the day chosen for this procedure.

"I've been wondering how each of us would spend this day," I told them, "and never imagined anything like this.".

A chaplain friend of mine arrived for a visit, and brought me a beautiful purple shawl.

"This is a Prayer Shawl," Theresa explained, "made by the Spiritual Care Volunteers of the hospital," where I had been volunteering as one of them for 6 years, but I had been unaware of the Prayer Shawl project.

She explained they pray as they knit the shawls, and she wrapped the gift of prayer around my shoulders and asked if she could pray with us. We formed a circle of prayer and she prayed very beautiful personal requests and statements of faith on my behalf. My daughter, Rosemary, was visibly frightened as she relayed how she had asked the cardiologist if I could die, and he told her it was a possibility. All I could say to her was, "This is a blessed day for us because of Chris, and it will continue to be a blessed day for us whatever happens."

Who was I kidding? We all knew we were all scared!

It was late morning when we were told the procedure would not take place until late afternoon. My crowd was getting larger as grandchildren arrived to join us. Thank God for our sense of humor! We were joking and laughing together on our blessed day. Early afternoon, while most of the family had gone for lunch in the cafeteria, the hospital priest came into my room. He talked with Rosemary and me and then asked if I would like his blessing. He is an elderly chaplain whom I've known for several years. I agreed, and he surprised me with an Apostolic Blessing and Absolution. What a beautiful gift on this anniversary day! It was especially reassuring for Rosemary.

Finally the cardiologist entered the crowded room to tell me he would now prepare to meet me for the procedure. He reviewed everything and then asked me, "Oh, by the way, what caused your son's death?"

I explained that he had apparently been born with a weakness at the root of his aorta, which had gone undetected all his life. "The coroner told us that is why he died so quickly but calmly in his sleep. The aorta had collapsed."

"Well," the cardiologist said as he turned towards my children and grandchildren in the room, "that is a hereditary condition that can now be detected in a test called an echo-cardiogram. I suggest you all have that test, because there is now medicine that can cure the condition your brother had. Not only siblings, but the next generation also should have echo-cardiograms."

Here, on the anniversary of Chris's death, his family had been gathered together in a way we could not have imagined, to receive news that could possibly save their lives.

At 4:30 p.m. I was put to sleep to have the stent put into my artery. I had again assured the nurse I did not want to be awake for the procedure, and I was immediately put to sleep.

Suddenly I woke up with a terrible painful tightening of my chest. I rolled my eyes around but saw no nurse. As the intense pain increased and spread down both arms so much that I thought I was having a heart attack, I saw the doctor sitting at the foot of the bed next to a technician. They were both watching the screen as the stent was being moved toward the blockage in my artery. My only thought was I had better not move or say anything to distract them! Then, quickly, the doctor said, "There it is! We got it!"

I watched the screen and saw the blood flow into the place that had been blocked, and immediately all the pain in my chest stopped. I had only been awake for a few seconds, but what a few seconds it was! It had been like watching new life start flowing in me. What an awesome experience! It was a God-filled time for me! I had actually watched my blood flow through my artery with new ease and assurance. I was breathing easily and relaxed and fell asleep.

That night, after my family left my hospital room, I closed my eyes and thanked God for the most beautiful day of life I could have experienced in memory of Chris. I felt immersed in gratitude for a life-giving day that I never could have planned or imagined. The next day I went home.

On the following Sunday, we all drove to the cemetery as we had planned. The weather was absolutely perfect, and the October colors were extremely brilliant on all the trees. Each one of us placed balloons and flowers of our choice on both graves, including all the small children solemnly putting their precious little bouquets there for Uncle Chris. Little Ben seemed drawn to sit next to the tombstone, tracing the letters of Chris's name with his little fingers. Then we all joined hands and prayed there in the sunlight, catching each others' eyes while praying. There was unexpected peace and comfort among us on that day!

We slowly walked away, leaving the beautiful flowers there with our balloons waving softly in the Autumn breeze. All the colors seemed brighter than possible. As we walked slowly away, quietly towards the pond, we each kept looking back. The children held our hands as we walked....and they too kept looking back

Gathering by the large pond, we sat on blankets and folding chairs, to share the food we had brought with us. The children enjoyed feeding the geese after we all relaxed and ate, and we talked of good memories of Chris, reflecting on how his happiest moments had been when we were all together for a meal. We had developed a family tradition of celebrating everything with a meal; whether the meal was at our dinner table, or camping...at a picnic table, on a blanket at the beach, at our backyard barbeques, or for holiday celebrations. We came together for meals always whether we were happy or when we were not so happy as after our Mass of The Angels, or following family funerals. It had grown to be something Chris took for granted whenever there was a reason to come together for a meal.

Now, as we prayed and ate and visited at the cemetary, we realized how blessed we were by his life and his love and the ways he brought us together.. We agreed to return on the next anniversary.

On October 5th, I boarded the plane for New York.

~~~~~~~~

When I think of you now, Chris........

I see you now as standing tall

strong and very straight

I see your reddish curly beard

with a smile still on your face

Your chest is full and very strong

Your shoulders now look wide

Your arms are very muscular

You're walking in long strides

Your hair the color it once was

a sort of reddish brown

You have a look of confidence

Where no one puts you down

I know you now can see and hear

I know your speech is clear

All pain is gone and you are strong

and I sometimes feel you near

I think of you as walking free

of winning a new race

of welcoming all others

to your beautiful Heavenly place......Love, Mom